Fodor's 2000

P9-CNI-854

Germany

Fodor's Travel Publications, Inc. • New York, Toronto, London, Sydney, Auckland

www.fodors.com/germany

CONTENTS

3

MAPS

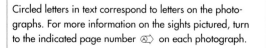

Circled letters in text correspond to letters on the photographs. For more information on the sights pictured, turn to the indicated page number Ⓐ on each photograph.

DESTINATION GERMANY

Every epoch has left its mark on Germany's landscape of fertile river valleys, rolling vineyards, and lofty peaks. Roman relics keep company with medieval castles, Baroque palaces with half-timbered farmhouses, and rococo urban mansions with communist-era housing. The country of oompah, cuckoo clocks, and Mercedes-Benz also gave the world Gutenberg, Luther, Bach, Beethoven, Goethe, and Marx. From the days of the Romans and Charlemagne through the Reformation to the present, it has been a tumultuous ride, and the start of the new millennium, marking the end of Germany's first decade of reunification, is a meaningful milestone. *Prost!*

MUNICH

Hands and beer steins down, the easygoing and fun-loving capital of Bavaria is the favorite city of both natives and visitors from abroad. Class and kitsch coexist amicably here—the former embodied in the glorious, half-mile-long Schloss Nymphenburg and the royal Ⓐ**Residenz,** home to Bavaria's art-loving Wittelsbach dynasty, and the latter the stuff of Ⓑ**Oktoberfest,** a fortnight-long tribute to beer and its consequences. Year-round, the *Gemütlichkeit* is nowhere stronger than in the city's many beer halls, of which surely the best-known is the venerable Ⓒ**Hofbräuhaus,** deafening and perennially packed. A much more tranquil refuge is Munich's 500-year-old late-Gothic Ⓓ**Frauenkirche,** whose twin domes are a city emblem. The gilded statue in

nearby Marienplatz was erected in 1638 by the Catholic city in gratitude for its deliverance from the devastating Thirty Years' War. Munich is also known for its superb galleries and opera house, and the lively restaurant scene is Germany's most sophisticated. Fashionable burghers shop on broad, ele-

gant Maximilianstrasse, de-
signed by King Maximilian II
himself, and in December ar-
tisans sell their wares at the
open-air ⒠**Christkindlmarkt** (Christmas Market). In the huge,
rolling Englischer Garten you can cross-country ski or sun-
bathe nude, depending on the season. And it's easy to hop on
the suburban railway to the lake resorts of the Ammersee and
Starnbergersee. The S-Bahn also reaches nearby Dachau, where
a Holocaust memorial tells the story of those who perished at the
concentration camp.

⒠ 75

BAVARIAN ALPS

Ⓐ 117

Germany is at its most photogenic in this area of majestic peaks, rocky pastures, and villages full of frescoed houses and window boxes bright with geraniums. Year-round you can find the country's finest skiing in Ⓑ**Garmisch-Partenkirchen,** and scenic hiking above mountain lakes

Ⓑ 94

such as fashionable Tegernsee, the quieter Schliersee, or the pristine Ⓐ **Königsee,** near Berchtesgaden. On an island in the Chiemsee is one of the palatial architectural fantasies of "Mad" King Ludwig II: Schloss Herrenchiemsee, modeled on Versailles. And once every decade in Oberammergau, noted for its wood-carvers, residents stage the Passion Play in celebration of the village's deliverance from the plague in 1633.

Perfect for hiking, biking, and cross-country skiing, this rural, wooded area of Germany next to the Austrian and Czech borders also stands out for its reasonable prices. From one of the low-key local country resorts you can make forays to small urban centers like arts-minded Deggendorff and river-crossed Ⓑ**Passau,** a Baroque gem. Stop in the city's magnificent

BAVARIAN FOREST

Ⓐ**Dom** at noon for a performance on the world's largest church organ. Or take in the Glasmuseum, showcasing treasures produced by an important local industry. Its focal point today is Zwiesel, but master glassblowers work in studios throughout the region. Also region-wide you can visit monasteries and churches adorned with the frescoes of 18th-century Bavarian artist Cosmas Damian Asam, one of a family of artists known for their stucco work and frescoes.

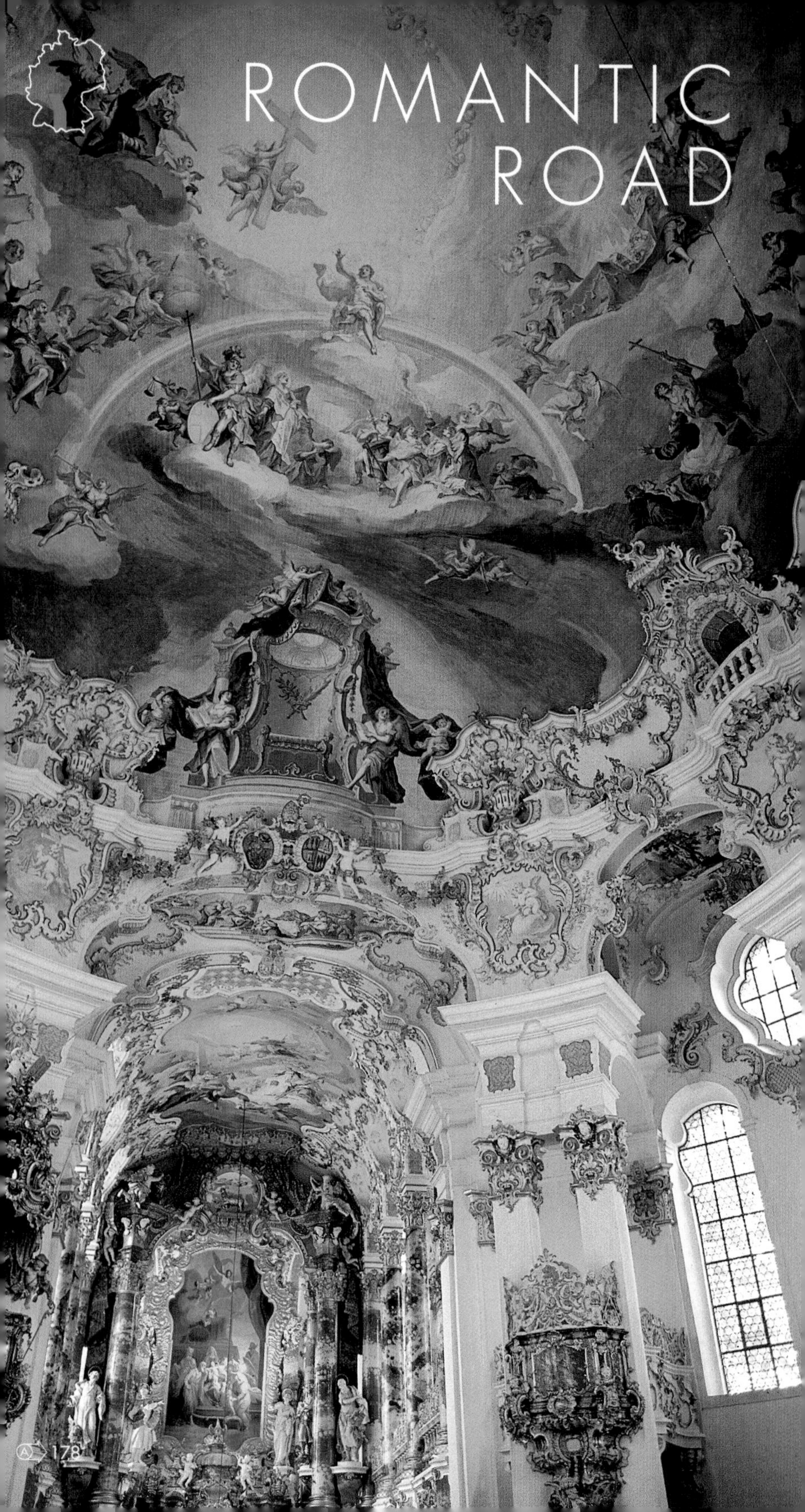

ROMANTIC ROAD

A 178

Picturesque beyond words, the Romantic Road is 260 miles of castles and walled villages, half-timbered houses and imposing churches, set in pastoral countryside. The art and architecture span centuries, and the rivers Tauber, Lech, Main, and Danube are never distant. Ⓓ**Rothenburg- ob-der-Tauber** is Europe's best-preserved medieval town, studded with turrets and towers. Ⓐ**Wieskirche,** in a meadow near Steingaden, is rococo.

Ⓞ 156

Ⓑ**Neuschswanstein,** Ludwig II's most famous castle, is pure 19th century—as romantic as they come. Soaring and light outside, it is sepulchral and Wagnerian within. At the Ⓒ**Residenz** in Würzburg, the Baroque era is at its best: the powerful prince-bishops who built it spared little expense in creating astonishing opulence. The Venetian Tiepolo painted its frescoes, including *The Four Continents,* above a remarkable split staircase by Balthasar Neumann. Augsburg was home to both the wealthy Fugger family and Marxist playwright Bertolt Brecht.

FRANCONIA

(A) 196

(B) 204

The region of Franconia is rich in ancient and cultural cities.
Opera fans love Bayreuth: The Wagner Festival thunders in
the stark Festspielhaus each summer, and the rococo (A)**Mark-
gräfliches Opernhaus** is an intimate jewel box. The lofty
Gothic (B)**Schöner Brunnen** (Beautiful Fountain) anchors the
market square of Nürnberg, artist Albrecht Dürer's longtime
home and site of the first diets of the Holy Roman Emperors. And
just outside Franconia is
(C)**Regensburg,** founded by
Celts on the Danube 2,500
years ago and remarkably
unscathed by World War II.

(C) 207

BODENSEE

Ⓐ⟩ 224

Ⓑ⟩ 221

The Bodensee, or Lake Constance, is the warmest area in Germany. The island of ⒸMainau defies the logic of latitude with displays of such exotic vegetation as lemon trees and hibiscus bushes. The scenery is enchanting, especially when viewed from shoreline promenades or from ferries traveling between towns like terraced Meersburg and beautifully preserved Konstanz, a half hour distant. The village of ⒶWasserburg, its castle now a hotel and its ancient streets off limits to cars, is a perfect contemplative retreat. So is the island town of ⒷLindau, whose history reaches back to Roman Gaul. Bike routes circle the lake; pedal long enough and you'll cross into Switzerland or Austria.

Ⓒ⟩ 237

Ⓐ 264

The Black Forest is synonymous with cuckoo clocks and primeval woodland: certainly thousands of acres are cloaked in pines, and at least one entire town, little Triberg, goes all atwitter every hour. But the storied Black Forest is at least as noteworthy for the beautiful people who flock to still-stately spa and casino resorts like Ⓑ**Baden-Baden** and the ultraluxurious Ⓒ**Schlosshotel Bühlerhöhe,** on a forested hilltop high above. And although pleasure is pricey here, not to worry: Elsewhere in the area, spa cures and mineral baths are far less costly—and the fresh, piney mountain air is free. There's boating and windsurfing on the Ⓓ**Titisee,** and hik-

BLACK FOREST

Ⓑ 253

Ⓒ 253

ers and cross-country skiers follow trails out of nearby Hinterzarten. Westward through the deep Hell Valley gorge is the beautifully restored university town of Freiburg, the region's largest city, with a cathedral, the Ⓐ**Münster,** that was 300 years in the making.

Ⓓ 261

HEIDELBERG AND THE NECKAR VALLEY

This is quintessential Germany—full of vineyards, castles, universities, and high-speed automobiles. In Ⓑ**Stuttgart,** swans are grace notes outside the Staatstheater, where the ballet and State Opera perform, and Porsche and Mercedes-Benz have factories just outside town. Nearby is the Burgenstrasse (Castle Road), which takes in castles and villages as it makes its way through the Neckar Valley. The castle ruins in Heidelberg, a gorgeous Baroque town on Gothic foundations, inspired the German Romantics. The best views of the old town are from the Ⓐ**Alte Brücke** (Old Bridge).

Ⓑ 291

15

Germany goes contemporary in Frankfurt. The city is now Europe's banking capital, a focal point of power. Germany's leading stock exchange, the Ⓑ**Börse,** is here. Skyscrapers spike the skyline, and prosperity has left the art museums flush with works by Dürer, Vermeer, Rembrandt, Rubens, Monet, and Renoir, among others. Jazz is popular, and the city has Germany's oldest jazz cellar as well as fall's annual German Jazz Festival. But not everything is modern. Römerberg Square is lined with historic buildings—the gabled Gothic Römer (City Hall) and

FRANKFURT

Ⓐ＞321

the row of half-timbered houses known as the Ostzeile. Frankfurters unwind in traditional ways, too: They head for the nearby Taunus Hills for a brisk hike and a bit of mountain air, or stop for an Apfelwein at *Ebbelwei* (cider taverns) such as Ⓐ**Adolf Wagner,** which punctuate the cobbled streets of quaint Sachsenhausen, on the south bank of the Main.

Ⓑ＞310

PFALZ AND THE RHINE TERRACE

Wine reigns here. Bacchanalian festivals pepper the calendar between July and October, and wineries welcome drop-ins for tastings year-round. Once you've had your fill of looking at the bottom of a wineglass, head for Worms, whose streets were ancient even when Charlemagne and Luther walked them. Its Ⓐ**Judenfriedhof,** Europe's oldest Jewish cemetery, has been in use for more than a millennium. The Wormser Dom is one of the world's great Romanesque cathedrals, along with the imposing Ⓑ**Kaiserdom** in Speyer and its fortresslike, turreted sibling in Mainz, the city where Johannes Gutenberg printed the first Bible.

Ⓐ 395

THE RHINELAND

Ⓑ 375

Although it is part of western-most Germany, the Rhineland is the country's spiritual heart. Stories that originated here—telling of the Nibelungen and the Lorelei—have become national legends, and tourists have been enthralled for centuries by the mighty Rhine as it flows past Koblenz, Köln, Bonn, and Düsseldorf, and the Ⓒ**Mosel,** the tributary that twists improbably past towns like Bremm. Their steep banks are graced with castles, villages, and vineyards: you can see them from your car or from one of the boats that cruise the rivers for anywhere from a few hours to as much as a week in season. Throughout the area

Ⓒ 389

Ⓔ⤳379

you can stay in castle hotels such as Ⓔ**Burg Gutenfels** near Oberwesel. Ancient Trier, on the Mosel, was 1,300 years old when Caesar's legions arrived, and its 2nd-century Ⓐ**Porta Nigra** (Black Gate) testifies to its importance to the Romans. Ⓕ**Wiesbaden,** on the Rhine, was founded by Roman soldiers who discovered the restorative properties of its hot springs, prized once again by 19th-century Europe's elite, who made this city the elegant place it is today. The world's best Rieslings are produced between here and half-timbered Ⓑ**Rüdesheim,** a bit downstream. The region's

Ⓓ⤳397

unofficial wine capital, Rüdesheim has plenty of cozy wine taverns. Farther north, in vibrant Ⓓ**Köln** (Cologne), a certain 18th-century eau de cologne is still for sale on Glockengasse at the address for which it is named, No. 4711.

However, the city may be most famous as the site of the country's largest and finest Gothic cathedral. Begun in the 13th century and completed in the 19th, it was intended to symbolize God's kingdom on earth, and it does so magnificently.

Ⓕ⤳372

THE
FAIRY-TALE
ROAD

The Fairy-Tale Road, stretching 370 miles between Hanau and Bremen, is also the Road Less Traveled. (All the better for those who choose it.) This is Brothers Grimm Country, the area that the great compilers of folklore mined for their sometimes-dark tales of magic and miracles. The Grimms' imaginations were nourished during a childhood in the ©**Brüder-Grimm-Haus** in Steinau an der Strasse, a medieval beauty of a town where

Ⓑ⟩ 423

their stories delight children today at the Ⓑ**Steinauer Marionettentheater.** In Ⓐ**Hameln** (Hamelin), sculptures, plaques, and even rat-shaped pastries recall the tale of the Pied Piper. And in Ⓓ**Bremen,** storied to have

Ⓒ⟩ 423

been saved by a quartet of animal musicians, drummers keep the beat during the pre-Lenten Carnival. All along the Fairy-Tale Road, misty woodlands and small towns full of half-timbered houses look as if they have mysterious and compelling tales to tell. When you pass this way, it's not hard to see how the area spawned the stories that the Grimms shared with the world.

Ⓓ⟩ 440

With its international port, rusty brick warehouses, fish market, and Reeperbahn red-light district, Hamburg is undeniably gritty. But its downtown is truly elegant. The area is laced with canals spanned by small bridges. The Inner and Outer Ⓐ**Alster,** bordered with parks and shopping arcades and big enough for sailing, form the

HAMBURG

city's heart, and a 9-mile footpath lines the Elbe River banks. Despite World War II bombings, the city's architecture is diverse, encompassing the neo-Renaissance Rathaus, on a square not unlike Venice's Piazza San Marco, and turn-of-the-century Art Nouveau buildings. The dining and arts scenes thrive, as well.

SCHLESWIG HOLSTEIN AND THE BALTIC COAST

Schleswig-Holstein and the former East Germany's Baltic coast area share a windswept landscape scattered with medieval towns, remote fishing villages, long white beaches, and summer resorts. The ©**Ahlbeck** pier dates from the 19th century, and charming Ⓐ**Stralsund** has a 13th-century redbrick Rathaus. Schwerin, the area's second-largest town after Rostock, has an amazing castle, and striking chalk cliffs edge remote, quiet Rügen island. In Schleswig-Holstein, major draws are chic Sylt island and medieval Lübeck, a stronghold of the powerful Hanseatic merchants who controlled trade on the Baltic beginning in the 13th century; the chunky gate known as the Ⓑ**Holstentor** recalls those days.

Ⓐ 500

Ⓑ 490

Ⓒ 506

BERLIN

For Germany, restored Berlin is an emblem of national renewal. More prosaically, *urban* renewal is everywhere. Massive construction projects have replaced the vanished Wall among the sprawling city's tourist attractions, right along with grand old sights such as the Berliner Dom, looming large over the Ⓐ**Spree Canal,** and the institutions of Museum Island, which display some of the world's best-known antiquities. The Ⓒ**Brandenburger Tor** (Brandenburg Gate), which stood in a no-man's-land in divided Berlin, is a reminder of the city's history. Tree-lined Ⓑ**Kurfürstendamm,** where Berliners congregate in cafés for cakes and coffee day and night, bristles with the energy that is the city's trademark.

Ⓑ⟩ 518

Ⓒ⟩ 519

SAXONY,
SAXONY-ANHALT
AND THURIGIA

Ⓐ 575

This area's difficult transition to capitalism is much in the news, but most striking to visitors are the reminders of the area's importance in history. Weimar was home to the poets Goethe and Schiller. The Bach family home and the Thomaskirche, where Johann Sebastian served as choirmaster for 27 years, are in Leipzig, where Richard Wagner was born. Both he and Richard Strauss had premieres at the imposing Ⓐ**Semperoper** (Semper Opera House) in Dresden, whose Brühlsche Terrasse above the Elbe River was once called "Europe's balcony." It was in Ⓒ**Meissen** that an 18th-century alchemist discovered how to make fine porcelain. And Martin Luther nailed his 95 theses to the door of Wittenberg's Ⓑ**Schlosskirche** in 1517, inching closer to a break with Rome. Near Eisenach you can also see the Wartburg fortress where the excommunicated Luther sought refuge.

Ⓑ 592

Ⓒ 579

GREAT ITINERARIES

Highlights of Germany
12 to 18 days

Germany offers everything from opera houses to oom-pah bands and from seaside villages to snowcapped mountains. For a parade of early German architec-ture, cruise the steeply banked, vineyard-terraced Rheingau between Mainz and Koblenz, full of river-side castles. The Romantic movement, a product of this evocative setting, flour-ished in the university town of Heidelberg. Munich, Germany's most laid-back city and the capital of Bavaria and of beer, is the gateway to the Alps and foothill lakes. In Nürnberg, relics of the Holy Roman Empire coexist with ruins of the Third Reich. Leipzig and Dresden are the pearls of what was East Germany, and, encap-sulating everything that is German, the restored capital of Berlin overwhelms with entertainment, culture, and reminders of 20th-century history.

the morning take a leisurely river cruise as far as Koblenz, breaking up your journey to overnight in a riverside Gasthof. Allow a day for exploring Koblenz, setting aside an hour to visit the scenic Deutsches Eck, the point where the Mosel flows into the Rhine, and the site of monuments to Germany's unity and division.
☞ *The Rhine Terrace in Chapter 10 and the Mittel-rhein in Chapter 11*

HEIDELBERG

1 to 2 days. Generations of artists, composers, writers, and romantics have crossed the Ⓐ Alte Brücke, spanning

in a centuries-old student tavern.
☞ *Heidelberg and the Neckar-Rhine Triangle in Chapter 8*

MUNICH AND THE ALPS

3 to 4 days. Visit Munich's Ⓒ Nymphenburg and Resi-denz, the former Wittelsbach palaces that demonstrate Bavaria's place in German history. Follow that with an evening in a beer hall, which will confirm everything you've ever heard about beer, pork, and potato consumption in Bavaria. Relax on the morn-ing train to Ⓑ Berchtesgaden, the Bavarian Alps a soothing cyclorama beyond the

Ⓐ 275

RHINE VALLEY FROM MAINZ TO KOBLENZ

3 to 4 days. From Frankfurt take the short train ride over the Rhine to see Mainz's Dom, one of Europe's great-est Romanesque cathedrals. Continue by train through Rheingau vineyards to Bingen and stay in a castle hotel. In

the Neckar River, and climbed up the steep, wind-ing Schlangenweg to the aptly named Philosophers' Path. At the top you'll have a view of Germany's arche-typal university city and its ruined Renaissance castle. Don't leave Heidelberg without eating (and drinking)

window. In Berchtesgaden Hitler's Obersalzberg retreat takes priority, but find time for the most beautiful corner of Germany, the mountain-ringed Königsee.
☞ *Chapters 1 and 2*

⑤ ▷114

NÜRNBERG

1 to 2 days. In Nürnberg you'll see the full spectrum of German history. The city's massive fortress, dating from 1050, was the residence of successive Holy Roman Emperors. The former home of Renaissance artist Albrecht Dürer is now a fascinating museum. Ride the S-2 suburban rail line to the Zeppelinfeld, the enormous parade grounds where Hitler addressed the Nürnberg rallies.
☞ *Southern Franconia and Upper Palatinate in Chapter 5*

LEIPZIG AND DRESDEN

2 to 3 days. To understand the enormous political and social changes brought about by German reunification you have to visit Leipzig or Dresden—both, if possible. Deteriorated after nearly a half century of communism, they have returned to commercial and cultural prominence. A choral concert in Leipzig's Thomaskirche, where Johann Sebastian Bach was choirmaster, or a walk high above the Elbe River along Dresden's Brühlsche Terrasse is completely enchanting.
☞ *Saxony in Chapter 16*

BERLIN

2 to 3 days. Reunited and rebuilt, Berlin races forward. The German parliament is back in the Reichstag, and world-renowned architects are changing the city's face. The Mittle district holds onto its pockets of counterculture as hip restaurants and bars move in. Sights recalling World War II and the Cold War are everywhere, and antiquities steal the spotlight on Museum Island. The Zoologischer Garten, Tiergarten, and Ku'Damm cafés offer the relaxation you'll need to balance this city's energy.
☞ *Chapter 15*

ⓒ ▷53

By Public Transportation
Mainz is a 30-min train ride from Frankfurt, and Bingen is 40 min farther by train or bus. Cruise boats leave Bingen daily for the Rhine journey to Koblenz. Catch an InterCity train in Koblenz for the return trip south, changing at Mannheim for Heidelberg (3 hrs). Return to Mannheim by a local train (10 min) and change to an InterCity or Eurocity train to Munich (about 3 hrs). InterCity Express and Eurocity services link Munich and Nürnberg (1 hr, 45 min). InterCity and InterRegio services link Nürnberg and Leipzig (3 hrs, 40 min) and Leipzig and Dresden (1 hr). There are hourly InterCity and other express services from Dresden to Berlin (1 hr). Return from Berlin to Frankfurt by InterCity Express (3 hrs) or fly back (40 min).

BRANDENBURG

Berlin

POLAND

SPREEWALD

190 km

A13

111 km

Leipzig

A14

Dresden

SAXONY

A9

Bayreuth

270 km

A9

Nürnberg

A9

BAVARIA

175 km

A9

A8

Munich

162 km

A8

AUSTRIA
Berchtesgaden

Castles in Wine Country
6 to 9 days

Centuries of German culture unfold on a medieval castle tour through the valleys of the Rhine and its tributaries. Today castle guest rooms and restaurants provide panoramic views as well as glasses of crisp Riesling and velvety Spätburgunder (pinot noir), Germany's finest white and red wines. ⒹWine estates often post signs near their entrances that announce WEINVERKAUF (WINE FOR SALE) or WEINPROBE HEUTE (WINE TASTINGS TODAY). Come during summer or autumn, when the wine-festival season is in full swing and many a castle courtyard hosts theater and concerts.

fairy-tale castle ⒺBurg Eltz. En route you'll pass breathtakingly steep vineyards and dozens of wine estates.
☞ *The Mittelrhein and the Mosel Valley in Chapter 11*

NECKAR VALLEY
2 to 3 days. Spend one day in Heidelberg's Old Town and massive castle ruins, but beware the crowds of summer. The town straddles the Hessische Bergstrasse and northern Baden wine regions. The white varietals Riesling, Grauburgunder (Pinot Gris), and Weissburgunder (Pinot Blanc) yield the finest wines. On the Burgenstrasse (Castle Road), have lunch on the castle terrace in Hirschhorn. Neckarzimmern's Burg Hornberg, residence of a celebrated 16th-century knight, is the perfect stopover.

Atop its own terraced vineyards in the Württemberg wine region, the 12th-century castle includes guest rooms with splendid views of the Neckar Valley as well as good food and wine (try the spicy white varietals Traminer and Muskateller). There's a museum and falconry at Burg Guttenberg, and medieval Bad Wimpfen has a former imperial palace.
☞ *Heidelberg and the Neckar-Rhine Triangle, and the Burgenstrasse in Chapter 8*

TAUBER AND MAIN VALLEYS
2 to 3 days. The Baden, Württemberg, and Franken wine regions converge in the peaceful Tauber Valley. Foremost are the earthy, robust, dry white Silvaner and Rivaner (Müller-Thurgau) wines, often bottled in the flagon-shaped Bocksbeutel. Bad Mergentheim, a pretty spa and former residence of the Knights of the Teutonic

MITTELRHEIN AND MOSEL
2 to 3 days. The Mittelrhein wine town of St. Goar is an ideal base for excursions into the Rhine and Mosel valleys. The terrace of the hotel-restaurant adjacent to Burg Rheinfels, the Rhine's largest fortress ruin, is a superb vantage point. Ferry across the river to catch a train to Rüdesheim, the liveliest town in the Rheingau wine region. Return to St. Goar on a KD Rhine steamer, and savor a glass of delicate Mosel wine or its fuller-bodied Rhine counterpart. Set aside a full day to tour the Rhine's only impregnable castle, the Marksburg, followed by a jaunt through the lower Mosel valley from Koblenz to the

Order, lies in the heart of the valley. In neighboring Weikersheim, tour the Renaissance hunting palace of the counts of Hohenlohe, after which you can sample the local wines in the shop at the gateway. Follow the course of the Tauber to its confluence with the Main River at Wertheim, also known as "little Heidelberg" because of its impressive hilltop castle ruins. In Würzburg, your next stop, you'll see many Gothic and Baroque masterpieces plus the Marienberg fortress and its successor, the Residenz. Three first-class wine estates here have wine pubs and shops.

☞ *Northern Romantic Road in Chapter 4*

By Public Transportation
Fast, frequent train service from Frankfurt to St. Goar, Koblenz, Heidelberg, or Würzburg, supplemented by local train and bus service, gets you to the above destinations within 2 hrs. The Deutsche Touring company's Europabus travels the Burgenstrasse, including Heidelberg and the Neckar Valley, as well as the Romantic Road, serving Würzburg, Bad Mergentheim, and Weikersheim. Sights are open and boats cruise the Rhine, Mosel, Neckar, and Main rivers from Easter through October.

The Great German Outdoors
7 to 10 days

Germans love the outdoors, and the autobahns are often jammed with families on their way to the countryside. News of a cold front on its way from Russia sets Germans to dusting off their skis, and the prediction of a high-pressure zone moving up from the Mediterranean fills the beds in hiking retreats. The mountains and lakes of Bavaria are Germany's playground. The Black Forest and Bodensee (Lake Constance), also in the south, are popular spa and recreation destinations. The gateway to all of them is Munich.

BAVARIAN ALPS AND LAKES
3 to 4 days. The Ammersee, ringed by cycling paths and walking trails, is a short ride from Munich. Most of the lakes in the Alps are warm enough for swimming in summer, and boatyards rent small sailboats and windsurfing boards. There are hiking trails in the mountains above Tegernsee; for more challenging walking head to Garmisch-Partenkirchen. It's one of Bavaria's three leading ski centers, with skiing virtually year-round on the glacier atop the Zugspitze, Germany's highest mountain. From here, wind your way down to the warmer clime of the Bodensee via the Deutsche Alpenstrasse.

☞ *Side Trips from Munich in Chapters 1 and 2*

BODENSEE
2 to 3 days. The Bodensee area is great for bicycling. In Friedrichshafen alone 25 hotels and pensions offer discounts if you arrive by bike, and an uninterrupted cycle path follows the north shore of the lake. In addition, the waters of the Bodensee offer the best inland sailing in Germany, and more than 30 boatyards rent everything from sailboards to cabin cruisers. The climate here is unusually

warm for Germany. Vineyards and orchards fill the hillsides, and rare and exotic plants decorate the tiny island of Mainau.

☞ *Chapter 6*

THE BLACK FOREST
2 to 3 days. The Black Forest has wide open spaces for walking, horseback riding, cycling, and even golf. In winter, meadows become ski slopes, and forest paths are meticulously groomed as cross-country ski trails. This is also spa country, where you can rest your weary limbs in hot springs like those in opulent ⒺBaden-Baden.

☞ *Northern Black Forest in Chapter 7*

By Public Transportation
The lakes near Munich are easily accessible both by S-bahn suburban services and via local trains that run hourly between Munich and Garmisch-Partenkirchen. The Bodensee towns are all within 3 hrs of Munich by train, and local buses and trains travel the north shore of the lake. Baden-Baden is about 6 hrs from Munich by train via Stuttgart or Karlsruhe, and 3–4 hrs from Friedrichshafen. Local buses and trains link Baden-Baden with most Black Forest resorts.

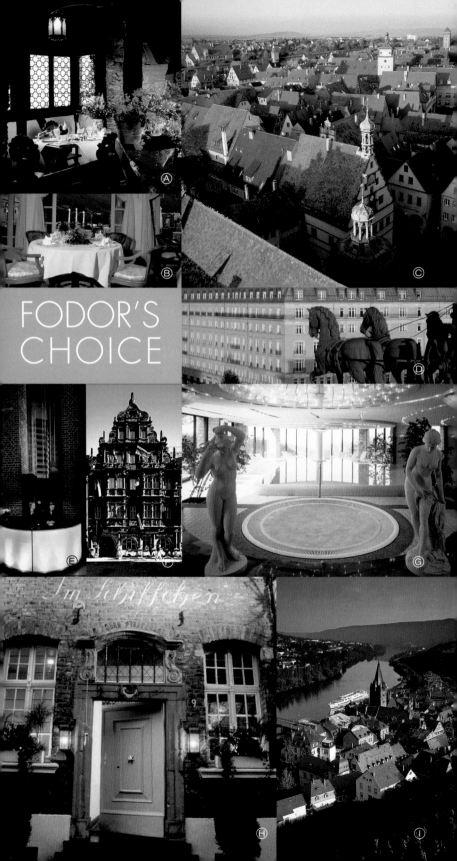

FODOR'S
CHOICE

Even with so many special places in Germany, Fodor's writers and editors have their favorites. Here are a few that stand out.

FLAVORS

Bareiss, Baiersbronn. The cuisine and champagne selection at this Black Forest mountain resort attract even the French from across the border. $$$$ ☞ p. 252

Ⓗ **Im Schiffchen, Düsseldorf.** Wear your jacket and tie for a special meal at this favorite of the Rhineland. The chef offers a lower-priced menu of local specialties at the ground-floor restaurant, Aalschokker. $$$$ ☞ p. 409

Ⓑ **Residenz Heinz Winkler, Aschau.** The reverence paid to herbs and spices here makes for sumptuous and healthy, French-leaning cuisine. Well-heeled Münchener's know the trip to Heinz Winkler's Alpine inn is worth it. $$$$ ☞ p. 111

Hotel-Restaurant Luther, Freinsheim. Handsome table settings and artistic presentation of imaginative meals make dining at this Baroque manor a joy for all the senses. $$$–$$$$ ☞ p. 354

Humperdinck, Frankfurt. Acclaimed chef Alfred Friedrich focuses his mastery on just 15 tables at a time in an intimate, neo-Baroque setting. $$$$ ☞ p. 316

Schiffergesellschaft, Lübeck. Share a communal oak table at a historic fishermen's tavern, and order whatever is fresh from the Baltic Sea. $$–$$$ ☞ p. 491

Grossbeerenkeller, Berlin. Berliners unwind over beer and Frau Zinn-Baier's famous fried potatoes in this cellar restaurant. $ ☞ p. 541

Wein- und Speisehaus zum Stachel, Würzburg. This restaurant in the Franken wine region's capital serves its own vintages and hearty Franconian fare. $ ☞ p. 157

COMFORTS

Dornröschenschloss, Sababurg. This castle is said to have inspired *Sleeping Beauty*. The small, luxury hotel is still surrounded by dense woods. $$$$ ☞ p. 432

Ⓓ **Hotel Adlon, Berlin.** No other hotel in Berlin can match the Adlon's history or its prestigious location near the Brandenburger Tor. $$$$ ☞ p. 543

Ⓔ **Hotel im Wasserturm, Köln.** Neoclassic on the outside, this onetime water tower has a sleek interior. $$$$ ☞ p. 404

Ⓕ **Romantik Hotel zum Ritter St. Georg, Heidelberg.** This charming Romantik Group hotel is in Heidelberg's only Renaissance building. $$$$ ☞ p. 280

Ⓖ **Schlosshotel Bühlerhöhe, Bühl.** High on a Black Forest mountain, this resort offers everything from aromatherapy and seaweed wraps to horseback riding. $$$$ ☞ p. 253

Vier Jahreszeiten Kempinski, Munich. This Four Seasons hotel known for luxury and excellent service is perfectly placed among the premier shops of Maximilianstrasse. $$$$ ☞ p. 63

Ⓐ **Auf Schönburg, Oberwesel.** This intimate hotel in a 1,000-year-old castle offers spectacular views of the Rhine from the terrace restaurant and many of the rooms. $$$ ☞ p. 379

Hotel Robert Mayer, Frankfurt. Artists have outfitted the rooms at the "Art Hotel" with unique flair. The style of most rooms within the 1905 Art Nouveau building is coolly minimalist. $$$ ☞ p. 322

Pension Hubertus, Bad Reichenhall. This family-run pension in the eastern Bavarian Alps gives you a taste of Bavarian hospitality and the chance to swim in or boat on a private lake. $ ☞ p. 114

MUSEUMS

Domschatzkammer, Aachen. In one of the richest cathedral treasuries in Europe is sacred art from late antiquity and the Carolingian, Ottonian, and Hohenstaufen eras. ☞ p. 406

Kunsthalle, Hamburg. German Romantic painters Caspar David Friedrich and Philip Otto Runge are featured here, as are masters like Holbein, Rembrandt, Van Dyck, and Tiepolo. ☞ p. 454

Museum der Bildenden Künste, Leipzig. A fine collection of Cranach the Elder's works is a highlight of the more than 2,700 paintings here. ☞ p. 585

Pergamonmuseum, Berlin. Within this museum are the Greek Pergamon Altar and other monuments of antiquity. ☞ p. 529

Wallraf-Richartz Museum and Museum Ludwig, Köln. The former's pictures span the years 1300 to 1900, with Dutch and Flemish schools particularly well represented, and the latter's 20th-century works include the heavy hitters of American pop art. ☞ p. 402

TOWNS WHERE TIME STANDS STILL

Bad Wimpfen. Romans founded this ancient hill town in the 1st century AD. The remains of Barbarossa's imperial palace and a picture-postcard ensemble of Gothic and Renaissance buildings are part of the town's marked walking tour. ☞ p. 288

Ⓘ **Bernkastel-Kues.** Late-Gothic and early Renaissance facades surround the market square of this Mosel River town. ☞ p. 391

Quedlinburg. A UNESCO World Heritage site, this Harz Mountains town has more than 1,600 half-timbered houses, the oldest dating from the early 1300s. ☞ p. 595

Ⓒ **Rothenburg-ob-der-Tauber.** This walled town on the Romantic Road is a treasure of medieval towers and turrets. ☞ p. 161

St. Martin. Grapevines garland ancient houses in one of the most charming wine villages of the Pfalz region. ☞ p. 345

Wasserburg. What was born as a fortress on the site of a Roman watchtower is now a car-free island town on the Bodensee. ☞ p. 224